Animals
HIDDEN
in the
FOREST

Jessica Rusick

PEBBLE
a capstone imprint

Published by Capstone Press, an imprint of Capstone
1710 Roe Crest Drive
North Mankato, Minnesota 56003
capstonepub.com

Library of Congress Cataloging-in-Publication Data
Names: Rusick, Jessica, author.
Title: Animals hidden in the forest / Jessica Rusick.
Description: North Mankato, Minnesota : Pebble, [2022] | Series: Animals undercover | Audience: Ages 5–8 | Audience: Grades K–1 |
Summary: "Some forest creatures are masters of disguise! They use camouflage and cover to outsmart predators or sneak up on prey. Some forest animals blend in with leaves, moss, and more. Others hide beneath rocks or in logs. Can you spot the creatures hidden in the forest?"-- Provided by publisher.
Identifiers: LCCN 2021041494 (print) | LCCN 2021041495 (ebook) |
  ISBN 9781666315455 (hardcover) | ISBN 9781666318128 (paperback) |
  ISBN 9781666315462 (pdf) | ISBN 9781666315486 (kindle edition)
Subjects: LCSH: Forest animals--Juvenile literature. | Camouflage (Biology)--Juvenile literature.
Classification: LCC QL112 .R84 2022 (print) | LCC QL112 (ebook) | DDC 591.73--dc23
LC record available at https://lccn.loc.gov/2021041494
LC ebook record available at https://lccn.loc.gov/2021041495

Image Credits
iStockphoto: i.fario, 25, milehightraveler, 29, 30, photobirder, 7; Shutterstock: Andrei Mayatnik, 23, Anna Veselova, 9, Artush, 3 (bottom middle), 10, 31 (middle), Attapol Yiemsiriwut, 20, 32 (top), Bruce MacQueen, 15, Cardaf, 1, 24, 32 (middle), critterbiz, 17, Jamikorn Sooktaramorn, 28, jWolskyPhotography, 5, Karen Hogan, 21, L-N, 3 (bottom left), 8, Merin Francis, 14, Mike Mulick, 3 (bottom right), 22, miroslav chytil, 11, RealityImages, 13, Ruth Swan, 26, 32 (bottom), Saichol Campan, 27, Tina Shaskus, 16, 31 (bottom), Tomas Drahos, Cover, Tom Reichner, 18, Vaclav Sebek, 12, Warren Metcalf, 6, 31 (top), yod67, 3 (top), Yuttana Joe, 19

Design Elements
Mighty Media, Inc.

Editorial and Design Credits
Editor: Rebecca Felix, Mighty Media; Designer: Aruna Rangarajan, Mighty Media

Printed in the United States   5324

HIDDEN IN THE
FOREST

Some forest creatures are masters of disguise! They use camouflage and cover to outsmart predators or sneak up on prey. Some forest animals blend in with bark, leaves, and more. Others burrow inside tree trunks or hide in leafy branches. Can you spot the creatures hidden in the forest?

First, try to spot the animal
hidden in the forest.

WHAT DO YOU THINK IT IS?

Turn the page to reveal the
animal and learn more about it.

DID YOU GUESS RIGHT?

This large rodent lives in trees and on the ground. What is it?

Turn and see!

IT'S A PORCUPINE!

Porcupines have long hairs with sharp tips. These are called quills. Quills help protect a porcupine. They can hurt predators during an attack!

This furry mammal has black markings around its eyes. What is it?

Turn and see!

IT'S A RACCOON!

Raccoons often make dens in hollow tree trunks. They come out at night to find food. Raccoons eat fish, nuts, fruit, and more.

This long lizard has a tail shaped like a leaf. What is it?

Turn and see!

IT'S A LEAF-TAILED GECKO!

Leaf-tailed geckos live in trees. They blend in with leaves and bark. Geckos have tiny, sticky pads on their feet. These pads help geckos climb.

This short-tailed wildcat has large paws. What is it?

Turn and see!

IT'S A **EURASIAN LYNX!**

Eurasian lynx are skilled hunters. They stalk prey from the cover of thick forest plants. Then, they attack! Eurasian lynx mostly hunt deer.

This crawly creature has eight legs. What is it?

Turn and see!

IT'S A TREE TRUNK SPIDER!

Tree trunk spiders have long spinnerets. These organs make silk. Tree trunk spiders use silk to catch prey. The spiders wrap insects in silk before eating them.

This furry rodent has long front teeth. What is it?

Turn and see!

IT'S A GROUNDHOG!

The front teeth of groundhogs grow quickly. Groundhogs chew on bark and grasses to wear these teeth down. The rodents also have sharp claws to dig burrows.

This hooved mammal is named for its tail. What is it?

Turn and see!

IT'S A **WHITE-TAILED DEER!**

White-tailed deer have a white patch under their tails. The animal raises its tail when it senses danger. The white patch is a signal. It warns other deer to be alert.

This forest mammal has webbed feet. What is it?

Turn and see!

IT'S A FLYING LEMUR!

Flying lemurs have flaps of skin between their limbs. This skin acts like a kite. It catches wind so lemurs can glide between tall trees. The lemurs also have sharp claws to grip bark.

This small bird has large yellow eyes. What is it?

Turn and see!

IT'S AN EASTERN SCREECH OWL!

Eastern screech owls often nest in tree holes. The owls eat fish, other birds, and more. They pounce from tree branches to catch prey. The owls store leftover food in their nests.

This amphibian with striped hind legs lives near water. What is it?

Turn and see!

IT'S A **COMMON FROG!**

Common frogs hunt at night. They have long, sticky tongues. The frogs use their tongues to catch slugs and snails.

This long-limbed bug hides in trees. What is it?

Turn and see!

IT'S A STICK INSECT!

There are many species of stick insects. Most species blend in with leaves and trees. This protects them from predators such as birds.

This flying bug can look like a leaf. What is it?

Turn and see!

IT'S A DEAD LEAF BUTTERFLY!

The dead leaf butterfly lives in Asian forests. It looks like a leaf when its wings are closed. This disguise helps the butterfly hide from predators.

This winged bug has a furry body. What is it?

Turn and see!

IT'S A WAVED SPHINX MOTH!

The waved sphinx moth is common in North America. Its markings help it blend into bark. The moths have long tongues. They use these to eat flower nectar.

FUN FACTS

Porcupines can have 30,000 or more quills!

A leaf-tailed gecko can lick its eyes to clean them.

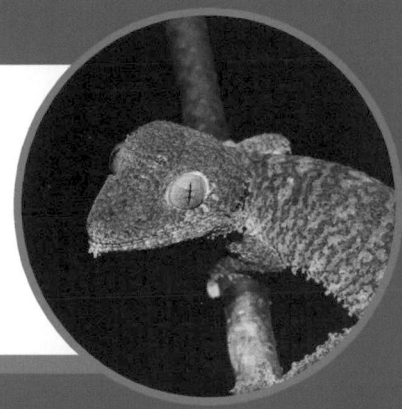

Groundhogs eat 1 pound (0.45 kilograms) of food per meal.

Flying lemurs have thin, light bones.

Common frogs can breathe through their skin.

Stick insects can detach and regrow their legs.